ORIGINAL CONFESSIONS

Of

MASTER NAT TURNER

The Complete Text of the Confessions of the
The Leader of the Most Successful Slave
Revolt in the United States of America

WITH A NEW, EDITED CHRONOLOGY
AND COMMENTARY BY

H. KHALIF KHALIFAH

Published by

UBUS COMMUNICATIONS SYSTEMS
26070 Barham Hills Road - Drewryville, VA 23844
www.khabooks.com - publish@khabooks.com
(434) 378-2140

1

FIRST EDITION - FIRST PRINTING
AUGUST 21, 2016
SECOND EDITION - FIRST PRINTING
JUNE 2, 2017

THE ORIGINAL CONFESSIONS OF
NAT TURNER by THOMAS R. GRAY
Edited with extensive commentary by H. Khalif
Khalifah & Nadirah U. Khalifah

ISBN# 1-56411-666-2   YBBG# 0673

PRINTED IN THE USA

By

LUMUMBA BOOK PRINTERS UNLIMITED
Post Office Box 1 - Drewryville, VA 23844
434-378-2140

CONTENTS

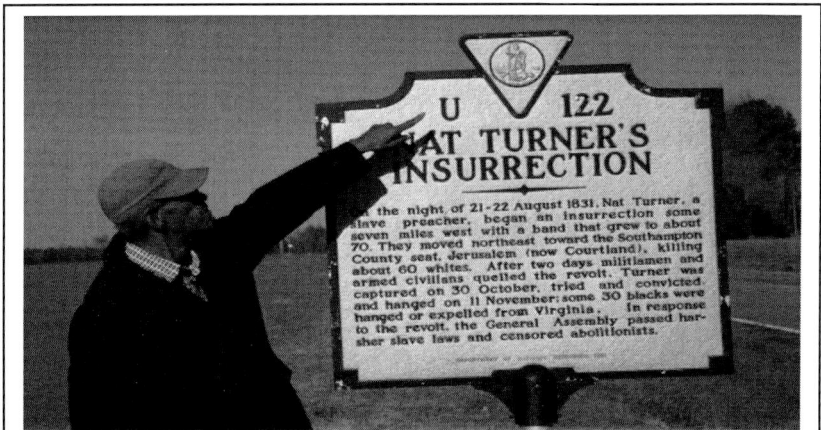

U 122

NAT TURNER'S INSURRECTION

On the night of 21-22 August 1831, Nat Turner, a slave preacher, began an insurrection some seven miles west with a band that grew to about 70. They moved northeast toward the Southampton County seat, Jerusalem (now Courtland), killing about 60 whites. After two days militiamen and armed civilians quelled the revolt. Turner was captured on 30 October, tried and convicted and hanged on 11 November; some 30 blacks were hanged or expelled from Virginia. In response to the revolt, the General Assembly passed harsher slave laws and censored abolitionists.

THOMAS R. GRAY:

Be it remembered, That on this tenth day of November, Anno Domini, eighteen hundred and thirty-one, Thomas R. Gray of the said District, deposited in this office the title of a book, which is in the words as following. The Confessions of Nat Turner, the leader of the late insurrection in Southampton, Virginia, as fully and voluntarily made to Thomas R. Gray, in the jail cell where he was confined. It was acknowledged by him to be such when read before the Court of Southampton, with the certificate, under seal, of the Court convened at Jerusalem, November 5, 1831 for his trial. Also, an authentic account of the whole insurrection, and with lists of the whites who were murdered, and of the negroes brought before the Court of Southampton, and their sentences & the rights whereof he claims as proprietor, in conformity with an Act of Congress, entitled, "An act to amend the several acts respecting Copy Rights."

THE CONFESSIONS OF NAT TURNER

Agreeable to his own appointment, on the evening he was committed to prison, with permission of the jailer, I visited Nat Turner on Tuesday the 1st November, when, without being questioned at all, he commenced his narrative in the following words:

SIR, - You have asked me to give a history of the motives which induced me to undertake the late insurrection, as you call it. To do so I must go back to the days of my infancy; and even before I was born.

I was thirty-one years of age the 2nd of October last. I was born the property of Benj. Tuner, of this county. In my childhood a circumstance occurred which made an indelible impression on my mind, and laid the ground work of that enthusiasm, which has terminated fatally to many, both white and black, and for which I am about to atone at the gallows.

It is here necessary to relate this circumstance. Trifling as it may seem, it was the commencement of that belief which has grown with time. Even now sir, in this dungeon, helpless and forsaken as I am, I cannot divest myself of.

Being at play with other children, when three or four years old, I was telling them something, which my mother overhearing, said it had happened before I was born. I stuck to my story, however, and related some things which went in her opinion, to confirm it. Others being told about it were greatly astonished. Knowing that these things had happened, caused them to say in my hearing, "I surely would be a prophet, as the Lord had shown me things that had happened before my birth."

My father and mother strengthened me in this first impression, saying in my presence, I was intended for some great purpose, which they had always thought from certain marks on my head and breast [a parcel of excrescence's which I believe are not at all uncommon, particularly among Negroes. I have seen several with the same. In this case he has either cut them off or they have nearly disappeared].

Nat Turner continues: My grandmother, who was very religious, and to whom I was much attached; my master, who belonged to the church, and other religious persons who visited the house, and whom I often saw at prayer meetings, noticing the singularity of my manners I suppose, and my uncommon intelligence for a child. They were heard to remark I "had too much sense to be raised, and if I was, I would never be of any service to anyone as a slave."

To a mind like mine, restless, inquisitive and observant of everything that was passing, it is easy to suppose that religion was the subject to which it would be directed. Although this subject principally occupied my thoughts, there was nothing that I saw or heard of to which my attention was not directed. The manner in which I learned to read and write, not only had great influence on my own mind, as I acquired it with the most perfect ease; so much so that I have no recollection whatever of learning the alphabet.

But to the astonishment of the family, one day when a book was shown to me to keep me from crying, I

7

began spelling the names of different objects). This was a source of wonder to all in the neighborhood, particularly the blacks.

This learning was constantly improved at all opportunities. When I got large enough to go to work, while employed, I was reflecting on many things that would present themselves to my imagination. Whenever an opportunity occurred of looking at a book; when the school children were getting their lessons, I would find many things that the fertility of my own imagination had depicted to me before. All my time, not devoted to my master's service, was spent either in prayer, or in making experiments in casting different things in molds made of earth.

I attempted to make paper, gun, powder and many other things with experiments. That although I could not perfect, yet convinced me of its practicability if I had the means.

I was not addicted to stealing in my youth, nor have I ever been. Yet such was the confidence of the Negroes in the neighborhood, even at this early period of my life, in my superior judgment, that they would often carry me with them when they were going on any roguery, to plan for them.

Growing up among them with this confidence in my superior judgment, and when this, in their opinions, was perfected by Divine inspiration, from the circumstances already alluded to in my infancy; and which belief was ever afterwards zealously inculcated by the austerity of my life and manners, became the subject of remarks by white and black.

Having discovered to be great, I must appear so: I studiously avoided mixing in society. I wrapped myself in mystery; devoting my time to fasting and prayer. By the time I arrived to man's estate; hearing the scriptures commented on at meetings, I was struck with that particular passage which says: *"Seek ye the kingdom of Heaven and all things shall be added unto you."*

I reflected much on this passage, and prayed daily for light on this subject. As I was praying one day at my plough, the Spirit spoke to me, saying "Seek ye the kingdom of Heaven and all things shall be added unto you."

QUESTION:

What do you mean by the Spirit?

ANSWER:

The Spirit that spoke to the prophets in former days. I was greatly astonished, and for two years prayed continually whenever my duty would permit. Then I again had the same revelation. This fully confirmed me in the impression: *that I was ordained for some great purpose in the hands of the Almighty.*

Several years rolled round in which many events occurred to strengthen me in this my belief. At this time I reverted in my mind to the remarks made of me in my childhood; and the things that had been shown me; and as it had been said of me in my childhood by those by whom I had been taught to pray, both white and black and in whom I had the greatest confidence, that "I had too much sense to be raised, and if I was, I would never be of any use to any one as a slave."

Now finding I had arrived to man's estate, and was still a slave, and these revelations being remembered, I began to direct my attention to this great object to fulfill the purpose for which, by this time I felt assured I was intended.

Knowing the influence I had obtained over the minds of my fellow servants, not by the means of conjuring and such like tricks; for to them I always spoke of such things with contempt), but by the communion of the Spirit whose revelations I often communicated to them; and they believed and said my wisdom came from God.

I now began to prepare them for my purpose, by telling them something was about to happen that would terminate in fulfilling the great promise that had been made to me. [If he said what the purpose was, and there is not a reason he would not have, John Gray did not record it].

About this time I was placed under an overseer, from whom I ran away. After remaining in the woods thirty days I returned. This was to the astonishment

10

of the Negroes on the plantation; they thought I had made my escape to some other part of the country as my father had done before.

But the reason of my return was that the Spirit appeared to me and said I had my wishes directed to the things of this world, and not to the kingdom of Heaven: that I should return to the service of my earthly master. *"For he who knoweth his Master's will and doeth it not shall be beaten with many stripes; and thus have I chastened you."*

The Negroes found fault, and murmured against me saying that: "if they had my sense they would not serve any master in the world."

About this time I had a vision. I saw white spirits and black spirits engaged in battle. The sun was darkened thunder rolled in the Heavens; Blood flowed in streams. I then heard a voice saying, *"Such is your luck, such you are called to see, and let it come rough or smooth, you must surely bare it."*

I now withdrew myself as much as my situation would permit from the intercourse of my fellow servants for the avowed purpose of convening the Spirit more fully. It appeared again to me, and reminded me of the things it had already shown me. It said that "it would then reveal to me the knowledge of the elements, the revolution of the planets, the operation of tides, and changes of the seasons."

After this revelation in the year of 1825, and the knowledge of the elements being made known to me, I sought more than ever to obtain true holiness before the great day of judgment should appear. Then I began to receive the true knowledge of faith. And from the first steps of righteousness until the last, was I made perfect; and the Holy Ghost was with me, and said, "*Behold me as I stand in the Heavens.*"

I looked and saw the forms of men in different attitudes. There were lights in the sky to which the children of darkness gave other names than what they really were. They were the lights of the Savior's hands - stretched forth from east to west,; even as they were extended on the cross on Calvary for the redemption of sinners.

I wondered greatly at these miracles and prayed to be informed of a certainty of the meaning thereof. Shortly afterwards, while laboring in the field, I discovered drops of blood on the corn as though it were dew from heaven. I communicated it to many, both white and black in the neighborhood.

I then found on the leaves in the woods hieroglyphic characters and numbers with the forms of men in different attitudes; portrayed in blood. They were representing the figures I had seen before in the heavens.

And now the Holy Ghost revealed itself to me, making plain the miracles it had shown me. For as the blood of Christ had been shed on the earth; and had ascended to heaven for the salvation of sinners; it was now returning to earth in the form of dew. The leaves on the trees bore impression of the figures I had seen in the heavens. It was plain to me that the Savior was about to lay down the yoke he had borne for the sins of men. The great day of judgment was at hand.

About this time I told these things to a white man (Etheldred T. Brantley) on whom it had a wonderful effect. He ceased from his wickedness; but was attacked immediately with a coetaneous eruption. Blood oozed from the pores of his skin. After praying and fasting nine days, he was healed, and the Spirit appeared to me again, and said; as the Savior had been baptized so should we be also.

When the white people would not let us be baptized by the church, we went down into the water together. This was in the sight of many who reviled us. We were baptized by the spirit. After this I rejoiced greatly, and gave thanks to God.

On the 12th of May, 1828, I heard a loud noise in the heavens. The Spirit instantly appeared to me. The Serpent was loosened and Christ had laid down the yoke he had borne for the sins of men. The Spirit said I should take it on and fight against the Serpent; for the time was fast approaching when the first should be last and the last should be first.

QUESTION:

Do you not find yourself mistaken now?

ANSWER:

Was not Christ crucified? By signs in the heavens It would make known to me when I should commence the great work. Until the first sign appeared, I should conceal it from the knowledge of men. On the appearance of the sign, (the eclipse of the sun last February) I should arise and prepare myself, and slay my enemies with their own weapons.

Immediately on the sign appearing in the heavens, the seal was removed from my lips. I then communicated the great work laid out for me to do. This was to four in whom I had the greatest confidence. (Henry, Hark, Nelson, and Sam).

It was intended by us to have begun the work on the 4th of July last. -Many were the plans formed and rejected by us. The planning affected my mind to such degree that I fell sick and the time passed without our coming to any determination about how to commence. We continued forming new schemes and rejecting them. When the sign appeared again. I was then determined not to wait longer.

Since the commencement of 1830 I had been living with Mr. Joseph Travis. He was to me a kind master. He placed the greatest confidence in me. In fact, I had no cause to complain of his treatment to me.

On Saturday evening, the 20th of August, it was agreed between Henry, Hark, and myself, to prepare a dinner the next day for the men we expected. We would then concert a plan, as we had not yet determined on any.

Hark, on the following morning, brought a pig, and Henry brandy; and being joined by Sam, Nelson, Will and Jack, they prepared in the woods a dinner, where, about three o'clock, I joined them.

QUESTION:

Why were you so backward in joining them?

ANSWER:

For the same reason that caused me not to mix with them in previous years.

I saluted them on coming up, and asked Will how came he there, he answered, his "*life was worth no more than others, and his liberty as dear to him.*"

I asked him if he thought to obtain it? He said "*he would, or lose his life.*"

This was enough to put him in full confidence. Jack, I knew, was only a tool in the hands of Hark. [Jack was about twenty years old and was the brother in-law of Hark).

it was quickly agreed we should commence at home (Mr. J. Travis') on that night. Until we had armed, equipped ourselves, and gathered sufficient force, neither age nor sex was to be spared (which was invariably adhered to). [We have reason to think Gray left out one of the marching orders that Nat Turner gave the men. That was the key command to Free the Captives and recruit them if possible].

We remained at the feast until about two hours into the night. When we went to the house we found Austin; he Joined us. They all went to the cider press and drank except myself.

On returning to the house Hark went to the door with an axe for the purpose of breaking it open. We knew we were strong enough to kill the family if they were awaked by the noise. But reflecting that it might create an alarm in the neighborhood, we determined to enter the house secretly, and kill them while they were sleeping.

Hark got a ladder and set it against the chimney. I ascended it and hoisted a window. I entered and came down stairs. I unbarred the door and removed the guns from their places.

It was then observed that I must spill the first blood. I was armed with a hatchet. I was accompanied by Will as I entered my master's chamber. It being dark, I could not give a death blow. The hatchet glanced from his head; he sprang from the bed and called his wife. These were his last words. Will laid him dead with a blow of his axe. Mrs. Travis woke up and shared the same fate.

The killing of this family, five in number, was the work of a moment. Not one of them awoke. There was a little infant sleeping in a cradle that was forgotten until we had left the house and gone some distance. Henry and Will returned and killed it. *[this is where, reportedly, Nat Turner said: "lice grow up to become nits." The baby was found later with his head bashed against the Chimney]*.

We got here, four guns that would shoot, and several old muskets and a pound or two of powder.

We remained some time at the barn where we drilled. I formed them in a line as soldiers. After carrying the men through all the maneuvers I was master of, I marched them off to Mr. Salathiel Francis'. He lived about six hundred yards distant.

Sam and Will went to the door and knocked. Mr. Francis asked who was there. Sam replied it was him, and he had a letter for him; on which he got up and came to the door. They immediately seized and dragged him out a little from the door. He was dispatched by repeated blows on the head. There was no other white person in the family.

[Salathiel Frances lived in the one room cabin with the one slave that he owned. It is thought his horrible profession may have been that of a "slave breaker." Gray does not record it, but all of the men wanted to

get a piece of him. The killing of Salatheil Frances may have been the only revenge killing. If he was, in fact, a slave breaker, he'd beaten and brutalized a lot of Captive Africans. His killing was the big payback. As I tell guest during the Nat Turner Trail tours: "They minced him; cut him up into little pieces"].

Nat Turner Continues:

We started from there for Mrs. Reese's. We maintained the most perfect silence on our march. Finding the door unlocked, we entered and killed Mrs. Reese in her bed while sleeping. Her son awoke but it was only to sleep the sleep of death. He had only time to say "who is that?" And he was no more. [the referenced Mrs Reese was Piety Reese, the owner of Cherry; Cherry was the wife of Nat Turner].

From Mrs. Reese's we went to Mrs. Turner's, a mile distance. We reached her house about sunrise on Monday morning. [this was the plantation house of Elizabeth Turner. She may well have been the widow of Benjamin Turner].

Henry, Austin, and Sam, went to the still, where, finding Mr. Peeples, Austin shot him, and the rest of us went to the house. As we approached the family discovered us and shut the door. Vain hope! Will, with one stroke of his axe opened it. We entered and found Mrs. Turner and Mrs. Newsome in the middle of a room almost frightened to death.

Will immediately killed Mrs. Turner with one blow of his axe. I took Mrs. Newsome by the hand, and with the sword I had when I was apprehended, I struck her several blows over the head but not being able to kill her, as the sword was dull.

Will turning around and discovering it, dispatched her also. A general destruction of property and search for money and ammunition always succeeded the killings.

By this time my company amounted to fifteen; the nine men mounted started for Mrs. Whitehead's with me (the other six were went through a by-way to Mr. Bryant's and were to rejoin us at Mrs. Whitehead's).

As we approached the house we discovered Mr. Richard Whitehead standing in the cotton patch near the lane fence. We called him over into the lane. Will, the executioner was near at hand with his fatal axe to send him to an untimely grave.

As we pushed on to the house, I discovered some one run round the garden; and thinking it was some of the white family, I pursued them. But finding it was a servant girl belonging to the house. The men I left had not been idle. All of the family were already dead, except for Mrs. Whitehead and her daughter Margaret.

As I came round to the door I saw Will pulling Mrs. Whitehead out of the house. At the step he nearly severed her head from her body with his broad axe.

Miss Margaret, when I discovered her had concealed herself in the corner formed by the projection of cellar cap from the house. On my approach she fled, but was soon overtaken. After repeated blows with a sword; I killed her with a blow on the head with a fence rail.

By this time the six who had gone by Mr. Bryant's rejoined us. They informed me they had done the work of death assigned them. On leaving the Whitehead's house, we again divided. Part going to Mr. Richard Porter's, and from thence to Nathaniel Francis'. The others went to Mr. Howell Harris', and Mr. T. Doyles.

On reaching Mr. Porter's he had escaped with his family. I understood then, that the alarm had already spread. I immediately returned to bring up those sent to Mr. Doyles, and Mr. Howell Harris.' The party I left went on to Mr. Francis.' I told them I would join them in that neighborhood.

I met those sent to Mr. Doyles' and Mr. Harris' returning. They had met Mr. Doyle on the road and killed him. They learned from some who'd joined them that Mr. Harris was away from home. I immediately pursued the course taken by the party gone on before; but knowing they would complete the work of death and pillage at Mr. Francis' before I could get there, I went to Mr. Peter Edwards' expecting to find them there. But they had been here also.

I then went on to Mr. John T. Barrow's. They had also been here and murdered him.

I pursued on their tracks to Capt. Newit Harris' where I found the greater part mounted, and ready to start. The men now amounted to about forty. They shouted and hurrahed as I rode up. Some were in the yard loading their guns. Others at the still drinking. They said Captain Harris and his family had escaped. The property in the houses they had already taken or destroyed, robbing him of money and other valuables.

I ordered them to mount and march instantly. This was about nine or ten o'clock Monday morning. We proceeded to Mr. Levi Waller's, two or three miles distant.

I took my station in the rear; and as it was my object to carry terror and devastation wherever we went, I placed fifteen or twenty of the best armed and most relied on in front. They generally approached the houses as fast as their horses could run. This was for two purposes: to prevent escapes and to strike terror into the inhabitants.

On this account I never got to the houses, after leaving Mrs. Whitehead's, until the killings were committed, except in one case. I sometimes got in sight in time to see the work of death completed. I viewed the mangled bodied as they lay in silent satisfaction.

21

We immediately started in quest of other slave owners. After killing Mrs. Waller and ten children, we started for Mr. Williams. We killed him and two little boys that were there. While engaged in this, Mrs. Williams fled and got some distance from the house but she was pursued, overtaken and compelled to get up behind one of the company. She was brought back, and after showing her the mangled body of her lifeless husband she was told to get down and lay by his side. She was shot dead.

We then started for Mr. Jacob Williams. There the family was already killed. Here we found a young man (named Drury who had come on business with Mr. Williams) He ran but was pursued, overtaken and shot.

Mrs. Vaughan was the next place we visited. After killing the family here, I determined on starting for Jerusalem. Our number amounted now to fifty or sixty. All were mounted and armed with guns, axes, swords and clubs.

[The army was as strong as it would become at this time. It was poorly equipped but if they managee to get to Jerusalem this would change. Nat Turner had men and women who were willing to do the work, but were not properly armed. Jerusalem is where the armory was located.]

Nat Turner continued:

On reaching Mr. James W. Parker's gate, immediately on the road leading to Jerusalem, about three miles distant, it was proposed to me to call there but I objected. I knew he was gone to Jerusalem. My object was to reach there as soon as possible. But some of the men, having relations at Mr. Parker's, it was agreed that they might call and get his people.

I remained at the gate on the road, with seven or eight. The others went across the field to the house about half a mile off. After waiting some time for them I became impatient and went to the house.

On our return we were met by a party of whites who had pursued our tracks. They had fired on the men left at the gate and dispersed them. I knew nothing of this, not having been rejoined by any of them.

Immediately, on discovering the whites. I ordered my men to halt and form as they appeared to be alarmed.

The white men, about eighteen in number, approached us to about one hundred yards. One of them fired, (this was against the positive orders of Captain Alexander P. Peete, who commanded, and who had directed the men to reserve their fire until within thirty paces).

And I discovered about half of them retreating. I ordered my men to fire and rush them. The few remaining stood their ground until we approached within fifty yards. Then they also fired and retreated. We pursued and overtook some of them. We left most of them dead (they were not killed).

After pursuing the remaining white men about two hundred yards, and rising a little hill, I discovered they were met by another party. They had stopped and were re-loading their guns...

(this was a small party from Jerusalem who knew the Negroes were in the field. They had just tied their horses to await their return to the road, knowing that Mr. Parker and family were in Jerusalem. They knew nothing of the party that had gone in with Captain Peete. On hearing the firing, they immediately rushed to the spot. They arrived just in time to arrest the progress of these barbarous villains and save the lives of their friends and fellow citizens).

Nat Turner continued...

Thinking that those who retreated first, and the party who fired on us at fifty or sixty yards distant, had all fallen back to meet others with ammunition; As I saw them reloading their guns. I saw more coming up than I saw at first. And with several of my bravest men being wounded, others panic struck and squandered over the field. The white men pursued and fired on us several times.

Hark had his horse shot from under him. I caught another for him as it was running by me. Five or six of my men were wounded, but none left on the field.

Finding myself defeated here I instantly determined to go through a private way.

This was to cross the Nottoway River at the Cypress Bridge three miles below Jerusalem. We were going to attack them from the rear. I expected they would look for me on the other road. I had a great desire to get to Jerusalem to procure arms and ammunition.

After going a short distance in this private way, accompanied by about twenty men, I overtook two or three who told me the others were dispersed in every direction.

After trying in vain to collect a sufficient force to proceed to Jerusalem, I determined to return, as I was sure they would make it back to their old neighborhoods. They would rejoin me after making new recruits and come down again.

On my way back, I called at Mrs. Thomas's, Mrs. Spencer's and several other places. The white families having fled. We found no more whites to fight. We stopped at Major Ridley's quarters for the night. We were joined by four of his men. These were the first recruits made since my defeat we mustered now about forty strong.

After placing out sentinels, I laid down to sleep, but was quickly roused by a great racket. Getting up I found some mounted, and others in great confusion. One of the sentinels had given the alarm that we were about to be attacked. I ordered some to ride round and reconnoiter. On their return the others became more alarmed, not knowing who they were. They fled in different ways. We were reduced to about twenty again. With this I determined to attempt to recruit more. We proceed to rally in the neighborhood.

Dr. Blunts' was the nearest house. We reached it just before day. On riding up the yard Hark fired a gun. We expected Dr. Blunt and his family were at Maj. Ridley's. I knew there was a company of men there. The gun was fired to ascertain if any of the family were still at home. We were immediately fired upon. We retreated leaving several of my men.

[According to Mr. James Magee, and in "reading between the lines" recorded by Thomas R. Gray, this was a great battles that is not adequately recorded anyplace in history I have read. The waiting whites in the house with guns; and, perhaps hundreds of Captives rushing the army on the ground defeated Nat Turner and the Black Liberation Army at the Blunt Plantation.]

Nat Turner recaps the aftermath of the battle:

I do not know what became of them, as I never saw them again. Pursuing our course back and coming in sight of Captain Harris' where we had been the day before, we discovered a party of white men at the house. On seeing this all deserted me but two, (Jacob and Nat).

We concealed ourselves in the woods until near night. I sent them in search of Henry, Sam, Nelson, and Hark. I directed them to rally all they could to the place we had had our dinner the Sunday before. They would find me there. I accordingly returned there as soon as it was dark.

I remained until Wednesday evening. When I discovered white men riding around the place as though they were looking for someone; and none of my men joining me, I concluded Jacob and Nat had been taken and compelled to betray me. On this I gave up all hope for the present. On Thursday night after having supplied myself with provisions from Mr. Travis's, I scratched a hole under a pile of fence rails in a field. There I concealed myself for six weeks, never leaving my hiding place but for a few minutes in the dead of night to get water which was very near. Thinking by this time that I could venture out, I began to go about in the night and eaves drop the houses in the neighborhood.

Pursuing this course for about a fortnight and gathering little or no intelligence, afraid of speaking to any human being, and returning every morning to my cave before the dawn of day. I know not how long I might have led this life, if accident had not betrayed me.

A dog in the neighborhood passing by my hiding place one night while I was out, was attracted by some meat I had in my hiding place. The dog crawled in and stole it. The dog was coming out just as I returned.

A few nights afterwards, two Negroes having started to go hunting with the same dog, and passed that way. The dog came again to the place, and having just gone out to walk about. The dog discovered me and barked. On which thinking myself discovered, I spoke to them to beg concealment. On making myself known they fled from me.

Knowing then they would betray me, I immediately left my hiding place. I was pursued almost incessantly until I was taken a fortnight ago by Mr. Benjamin Phipps. I was hiding in a little hole I had dug out with my sword, for the purpose of concealment, under the top of a fallen tree.

On Mr. Phipps' discovering the place of my concealment, he cocked his gun and aimed at me. I requested him not to shoot and I would give up, upon which he demanded my sword. I delivered it to him, and he brought me to prison.

During the time I was pursued, I had many hair breadth escapes, which your time will not permit you to relate. I am here loaded with chains, and willing to suffer the fate that awaits me.

(INTERVIEWER: I here proceeded to make some inquiries of him. I assured him of the certain death that awaited him; and that concealment would only bring destruction on the innocent as well as guilty, of his own color. I wanted to know if he knew of any extensive or concerted plan.

His answer was "I do not."

When I questioned him as to the insurrection in North Carolina happening about the same time, he denied any knowledge of it; and when I looked him in the face as though I would search his inmost thoughts, he replied:

"I see sir, you doubt my words; but can you not think the same ideas, and strange appearances at one time; the heaven's might prompt the same in others, as well as myself, to this undertaking."

I now had much conversation with him and asked him many questions, having forborne to do so previously, except in the cases noted in parenthesis. But during his statement, I had, unnoticed by him, taken notes as to some particular circumstances. Now having the advantage of his statement before me in writing, on the evening of the third day that I had been with him, I began a cross examination, and found his statement corroborated by every circumstance coming within my own knowledge or the confessions of others who had been either killed or executed, and whom he had not seen nor had any knowledge since 22nd of August last.

He expressed himself, fully satisfied as to the impracticability of an attempt to evade. It has been said he was ignorant and cowardly; and that his object was to murder and rob for the purpose of obtaining money to make his escape. It is notorious that he was never known to have a dollar in his life; to swear an oath, or drink a drop of spirits.

As to his ignorance, he certainly never had the advantages of education, but he can read and write, (it was taught him by his parents), and for natural intelligence and quickness of apprehension, is surpassed by few men I have ever seen.

As to his being a coward, his reason was given for not resisting Mr. Phipps, shows the decision of his character. When he saw Mr. Phipps present his gun, he said he knew it was impossible for him to escape as the woods were full of men. He therefore thought it was better to surrender, and trust to fortune for his escape.

He is a complete fanatic, or plays his part most admirably. On other subjects he possesses an uncommon share of intelligence. He has a mind capable of attaining anything but warped and perverted by the influence of early impressions.

He is below the ordinary stature, though strong and active, having the true Negro face, every feature of which is strongly marked. I shall not attempt to describe the effect of his narrative, as told and commented on by himself, in the condemned hole of the prison.

The calm, deliberate composure with which he spoke of his late deeds and intentions; the expression of his fiend-like face when excited by enthusiasm, still bearing the stains of the blood of helpless innocence about him; clothed with rags and covered with chains; yet daring to raise his manacled hands to heaven with a spirit soaring above the attributes of man;. I looked on him and my blood curdled in my veins.

I will not shock the feelings of humanity, nor wound afresh the bosoms of the disconsolate sufferers in this unparalleled and inhuman massacre by detailing the deeds of their fiend-like barbarity.

There were two or three who were in the power of these wretches, had they known it, and who escaped in the most providential manner. There were two whom they thought they left dead on the field at Mr. Parker's, but who were only stunned by the blows of their guns, as they did not take time to re-load when they charged on them.

The escape of a little girl who went to school at Mr. Waller's, and where the children were collecting for that purpose, excited general sympathy. As their teacher had not arrived, they were at play in the yard, and seeing the Negroes approach, she ran up on a dirt chimney, (such as are common to log houses,) and remained there unnoticed during the massacre of the eleven that were killed at this place. She remained in her hiding place till just before the arrival of a party, who were in pursuit of the murderers, when she came down and fled to a swamp where, a mere child as she was, with the horrors of the late scene before her, she lay concealed until the next day, when seeing a party go up to the house, she came up, and on being asked how she escaped, replied with the utmost simplicity, "The Lord helped her."

She was taken up behind a gentleman of the party, and returned to the arms of her weeping mother. Miss Whitehead concealed herself between the bed and the mat that supported it while they murdered her sister in the same room without discovering her. She was afterwards carried off, and concealed for protection by a slave of the family, who gave evidence against several of them on their trial.

Mrs. Nathaniel Francis, while concealed in a closet heard their blows, and the shrieks of the victims of these ruthless savages; they entered the closet where she was concealed, and went out without discovering her. While in this hiding place, she heard two of her women in a quarrel about the division of her clothes.

Mr. John T. Barrow, discovering them approaching his house, told his wife to make her escape, and scorning to fly, fell fighting on his own threshold. After firing his rifle, he discharged his gun at them, and then broke it over the villain who first approached him, but he was overpowered, and slain. His bravery, however, saved from the hands of these monsters, his lovely and amiable wife, who will long lament a husband so deserving of her love. As directed by him, she attempted to escape through the garden, when she was caught and held by one of her servant girls, but another coming to her rescue, she fled to the woods, and concealed herself.

Few indeed, were those who escaped their work of death. But fortunate for society, the hand of retributive justice has overtaken them; and not one that was known to be concerned has escaped.

[The success of The Nat Turner and BLA Revolt of 1831 makes the contradictory commentaries of John R. Gray laughable.

The "innocent lives" that he laments that were taken by Nat Turner, were chattel slave holding white people who brutalized and murdered innocent Black people.

His assertion that "retributive Justice has overtaken them" was a vain attempt to allay the fears of white people.

Clearly Justice is on the side of the innocent and there can never be anything innocent about a man or woman who claims ownership of another human being.

Furthermore, some Black Captives made a safe retreat back to the "neighborhoods," as Nat Turner called their home plantations; and the many the state sold out of state effectively spread information about the revolt.

Gray extols the intelligence and virtues of Nat Turner in several places in "The Confessions," saying, "I have met few who surpassed his intellect." Then we read the laborious butchery he does in recording the words of the intelligence of Nat Turner.

Though Nat Turner was a Freedom Fighter par excellence, Gray took considerable pain to never attribute motives for the Revolt. It was to Free Black people from chattel bondage.

The soldiers he vainly tried to revile by calling them murderers throughout the "Confessions" strains the imagination to think anyone could ever call the killing of a slave owner for our stolen Freedom Justice & Equality a murderer.

The people he tried to castigate as murderers and barbarians were of the same people he recounts in several instances whom saved their white owners by concealing them from Nat Turner.

Gray left out certain things that Nat Turner surely talked about. Things like his reasons for making a decision at one time to turn himself in. There is little doubt that he knew about the slaughter white people were carrying out against Black People. At one time He thought that giving himself up may bring it to an end].

THE TRIAL & DISPOSITION OF NAT TURNER AND THE BLACK LIBERATION ARMY

THE COMMONWEALTH VS NAT TURNER

Charged with making insurrection and plotting to take away the lives of free white persons.

 The court composed of _____, having met for the trial of Nat Turner. The prisoner was brought in and arraigned, and upon his arraignment pleaded not guilty, saying to his counsel that he did not feel so.

 On the part of the Commonwealth, Levi Waller was introduced, who being sworn, deposed as follows: (agreeably to Nat's own confession), Col. Trezant (The Committing Magistrate) was then introduced, who being sworn, narrated Nat's Confession to him, as follows. (his Confession as given to Mr. Gray). The prisoner was produced as evidence, and the case was submitted without augment to the court, who having found him guilty, Jeremiah Cobb, Esq. Chairman, pronounced the sentence of the court, in the following words: "Nat Turner! Stand up! Have you anything to say why sentence of death should not be pronounced against you?"

ANSWER:

"I have not. I have made a full confession to Mr. Gray, and I have nothing more to say."

Attend then to the sentence of the court. You have been arraigned and tried before this court and convicted of one of the highest crimes in our criminal code. You have been convicted of plotting in cold blood, the indiscriminate destruction of men, of helpless women, and of infant children. The evidence before us leaves not a shadow of doubt but that your hands were often imbued in the blood of the innocent; and your own confession tells us that they were stained with the blood of the master, in your own language, 'too indulgent.'

Could I stop here your crime would be sufficiently aggravated. But the original contriver of a plan, deep and deadly, one that never can be effected, you managed so far to put it into execution, as to deprive us of many of our most valuable citizens; and this was done when they were asleep, and defenseless, under circumstances shocking to humanity. And while upon this part of the subject, I cannot but call your attention to the poor misguided wreches who have gone before you. They are not few in number: they were your bosom associates; and the blood of all cries aloud, and calls upon you, as the author of their misfortune. Yes! You forced them unprep[ared. From time to Eternity. Borne down by this load of guilt, your only justification is that ou were led away by fanaticism. If this is true, from my soul I pity you; and while you have my Sympaties, I am nevertheless called on to pass the sentence of the court. The time between now and your execution will necessarily be very short. Your only hope must be in another world. The judgment of the court is that you be taken hence to the jail from whence you came, thence to the place of your execution, and on Friday next, between the hours of 10 a. m. and 2 p.m. be hung by the neck until you are dead! Dead! Dead! And may the Lord have mercy upon your soul.

[The dribble of white slave owners never cease to amaze, and never cease to sickened. Just to know that humans, thelikes of Judge Cobb can be so callous as think the freedom they claim to cherish for themselves is not cherished more so by Black people].

THE FOLLOWING MEMBERS OF THE BLACK LIBERATION ARMY MEMBERS WERE TRIED AND DISPOSTITION AS INDICATED.

They were all tried in the "Slave Court" called Oyer Terminger. Nat Turner was tried in Circuit Court.

Full Trial Transcripts: Southampton County Court of Oyer and Terminer, Aug. 31-Nov. 21, 1831

Trial of Daniel (slave of Richard Porter), August 31, 1831 – Executed
Trial of Tom (slave of Caty Whitehead estate), August 31, 1831 – Discharged
Trial of Jack (slave of Caty Whitehead estate), September 1, 1831 – Transported
Trial of Andrew (slave of Caty Whitehead estate), September 1, 1831 – Transported
Trial of Moses (slave of Thomas Barrow estate), September 1, 1831 – Executed

Trial of Davy (slave of Elizabeth Turner estate), September 2, 1831 –
Executed
Trial of Curtis (slave of Thomas Ridley), September 2, 1831 – Executed
Trial of Stephen (slave of Thomas Ridley), September 2, 1831 –
Executed
Trial of Isaac (slave of George H. Carlton, Greenville County),
September 2, 1831 – Transported
Trial of Sam (slave of Nathaniel Francis), September 3, 1831 – Executed
Trial of Hark (slave of Joseph Travis estate), September 3, 1831 –
Executed
Trial of Nelson (slave of Jacob Williams), September 3, 1831 –
Executed
Trial of Davy (slave of Levi Waller), September 3, 1831 – Executed
Trial of Nat (slave of Edwin Turner estate), September 3, 1831 –
Executed
Trial of Jack (slave of William Reese estate), September 5, 1831 –
Executed
Trial of Dred (slave of Nathaniel Francis), September 5, 1831 –
Executed
Trial of Arnold Artest (free man of color), September 5, 1831 –
Discharged
Trial of Nathan (slave of Benjamin Blunt estate), September 6, 1831 –
Executed
Trial of Nathan, Tom, & Davy (slaves of Nathaniel Francis), September
6, 1831 – Transported
Trial of Hardy (slave of Benjamin Edwards), September 7, 1831 –
Transported
Trial of Isham (slave of Benjamin Edwards), September 7, 1831 –
Transported
Trial of Sam (slave of James W. Parker), September 7, 1831 –
Discharged
Trial of Jim (slave of William Vaughan), September 7, 1831 –
Discharged
Trial of Bob (slave of Temperance Parker), September 8, 1831 –
Discharged
Trial of Davy (slave of Joseph Parker), September 8, 1831 – Discharged
Trial of Daniel (slave of Solomon Parker), September 8, 1831 –
Discharged
Trial of Joe (slave of John C. Turner), September 19, 1831 – Executed

Trial of Lucy (slave of John T. Barrow estate), September 19, 1831 – Executed

Trial of Matt (slave of Thomas Ridley), September 19, 1831 – Discharged

Trial of Thomas Haithcock (free man of color), September 19, 1831 – Superior Court

Trial of Jim (slave of Richard Porter), September 19, 1831 – Discharged

Trial of Barry Newsom (apprentice of Peter Edwards), September 20, 1831 – Superior Court

Trial of Jack (slave of Everett Bryant), September 20, 1831 – Discharged

Trial of Exum Artist (free man of color), September 20, 1831 – Superior Court

Trial of Stephen (slave of James Bell), September 21, 1831 – Discharged

Trial of Jim & Isaac (slaves of Samuel Champion), September 22, 1831 – Transported

Trial of Preston (slave of Hannah Williamson), September 22, 1831 – Discharged

Trial of Frank (slave of Solomon Parker), September 22, 1831 – Transported

Trial of Nelson (slave of Benjamin Blunt estate), September 28, 1831 – Discharged

Trial of Jack & Shadrach (slave of Nathaniel Simmons), September 28, 1831 – Discharged

Trial of Sam (slave of Peter Edwards), September 28, 1831 – Executed

Trial of Archer (slave of Arthur G. Reese), October 18, 1831 – Discharged

Trial of Isham Turner (free man of color), October 18, 1831 – Superior Court

Trial of Moses (slave of Joseph Travis estate), October 18, 1831 – Transported

Trial of Nat, alias Nat Turner (slave of Putnam Moore, deceased), November 5, 1831 – Executed

Trial of Ben (slave of Benjamin Blunt estate), November 21, 1831 – Executed

Trial of Isham Turner (free man of color), October 18, 1831 – Superior Court

Trial of Moses (slave of Joseph Travis estate), October 18, 1831 – Transported

Trial of Nat, alias Nat Turner (slave of Putnam Moore, deceased), November 5, 1831 – Executed
Trial of Ben (slave of Benjamin Blunt estate), November 21, 1831 – Executed

AFTERWORDS

EDITING A HISTORIC DOCUMENT CALLED "THE CONFESSIONS OF NAT TURNER"

WHAT IS THE NAT TURNER LIBRARY?

The Nat Turner Library is within the Nat Turner Library Building. It is located on a 123 acre tract of the birth land of Nat Turner. The Mission of the Independent Black Institution is to do things necessary to "Correct, Preserve and Propagate" the legacy and work of Nat Turner and the Black Liberation Army that he organized and led in August of 1831. It also proposes to do the same for other Black individuals who will not receive their just due for making contributions to the survival of a Noble Freedom Bound People.

Primarily, we treat Black nationalist, Black Muslims, Pan Africanist and other Black people living and dead, who saw independence from White Supremacist based systems as the requisite for Freedom . But we certainly do not limit repositories to the like of Dr. Amos N. Wilson and Queen Mother Moore.

What is the short answer as to why we would edit the historic document called The Confessions of Nat Turner?

The only humans who know what Nat Turner said was Nat Turner and Thomas R. Gray. However, there are some things that Thomas R. Gray wrote that we know is not what Nat Turner said, or the way he said them; let alone what he meant. But we submit that Mystic that he was and as determined as he happened to be, Nat Turner answered Grays questions to refute Grays efforts to mischaracterize him and the Revolt that he led.

Editing the Confessions of Nat Turner is intended to identify & clarify his reason for agreeing to be interviewed. Nat Turner wanted to give a correct account of the revolt that he led. The correct account has lessons that he wanted to convey to the people that he attempted to liberate. We intend to make it easier to "read between the lines" to see the lessons.

We are also certain that Nat Turner wrote a summary report during his some 60 Freedom Days following the aborted revolt. Until his account is found, the closest we'll come to know the lessons is to "read between the lines" of what Mr. Thomas R. Gray claims Nat Turner said: our editing and commentary propose to help with that.

Also key to fulfilling our Mission are the Nat Turner Trail Tours; as well as other activities at KKVV.

Our Introduction is also to show the Standard Living History Tour. And some information about the work of Nat Turner & the Black Liberation Army of 1831.

STANDARD NAT TURNER TRAIL TOUR

Retracing Part Of The Approximate Route Of Nat Turner And The Black Liberation Army Of 1831

INSIDE THE KKVV PROGRAM GUIDE
• A Universal Meditation/Prayer
• Trial Transcript of the BLA Members organized and led by Nat Turner in 1831 page 6 & 7
• List of Members of BLA 1831 that were caught & Tried
• Application for the KKVV ManUp Camp Rites of Passage into Black Manhood - Contact Information page 8

THE TOUR BEGINS:

1. The Nat Turner Library Building & Bookstore
2. Go to church reputedly founded by Slave Owner Benjamin in 1786. Nat Turner allegedly preached here.
3. Plantation/Battle site of Joseph Travis. Nat Turner's Owner Putnam Moore Jr lived here (6)
4. Plantation/Battle site of Possibly "Slave Breaker" Salathiel Frances minced here by entire army (1)
5. Visit Home to home of Nat Turner descendant Alvin Turner & his wife Evangeline.
6. Visit battle Site of Piety Reese. Nat Turner's Wife Cherry's Owner lived here (4). As a child Alvin Turner lived at this site.
7. Visit Battle Site of Elizabeth Turner (5). Afterwards, A detail was sent to the Bryant (4) and Francis Plantations (6)
8. Visit Cabin Pond; Cabin Pond was the staging area on August 21 where a Final Battle Plan was decided; invited to meeting were Sam, Nelson, Hark, Henry. Will the Executioner & Jack were brought.
9. Visit Plantation House and Cemetery of Richard Porter.
10. The Battle Site of Margaret Whitehouse. The only killing claimed by Nat Turner happened here (6)
11. Visit Marker about the revolt at Cross Keys
12. Drive by the site of the Southampton Auction Block and Jailhouse in 1831
13. Drive by Blackhead Sign Post Road
14. Drive by the Parker Plantation; two miles from Jerusalem.
15. Go to The current Jailhouse and the Courthouse where Nat Turner was tried
16. Visit restored Plantation House of Rebecca Vaughn

17. Visit to the place where the Hanging Tree was in 1831
18. Go to the Marker that white people celebrate those "faithful slave that helped to defeat Nat Turner in 1831."
19. Return to the Nat Turner Library for a debriefing, dinner, discussion questions and answers.

A UNIVERSAL MEDITATION/PRAYER

Surely We turn ourselves, being upright to He who originated the Universal of All, Persons, Places & Things
We are not polytheist
But we have been deeply unjust to ourselves
In that we have not mastered the Laws of Maat
Not having mastered the Melanin Law of the Universe
We make mistakes, we go into error & we indulge in excesses

So we seek refuge in Thee from all of our faults
For none can grant refuge against faults but Thou
In the State of Amen the State in which we were
Created within as divine Beings

On this day and forever
We will execute our Words, Acts & Deeds
As the divine Beings we were created to be
They will be spoken, enacted & intended
As the divine Beings we are striving to be
As we take care of Our Duties & Our Responsibilities to our children, to our grandchildren, to our mates, to our future mates as well as to those who meditate at the hour of eight

Bless those who are with us, bless the ones with sincere desires to be and Bless others who may be coming into our experiences, on this day and forever........ASE!

[The above was taken from the book, "Mastering the Laws of Creation: Introduction to Melanin Science]

44

Top: drawing of Nat Turner: Middle Senior Khalifah at cross Marker; Bottom; Nat Turner Library Building. Call 434-378-2140 for booking support

INFORMATION ABOUT THE BATTLE SITES
NOT VISITED ON STANDARD TOURS

The Bryant Plantation (4). After the division of the army the detail on foot defeated the Bryant Plantation and...

Nathaniel Frances (6). They couldn't stamp out the bloodline because Slaveowner, Nathanial Francis was not at home. They missed his wife Lavinia as slaves hid her in the attic.

The Howell Plantation; the family was gone but they met a fellow named Trajan Doyle in the road and killed him (1)

The John Barrow Plantation. Barrow knew the army was coming. He sent his wife away but stayed home. He fought bravely but lost. The army left a commendation: (1)

The Newit Harris Plantation; nobody home (0)

The Levi Waller Plantation. Mrs Waller killed along with ten others (11). Waller hid in the woods and watched the BLA work on his wife and children. He Testified about his observations at many subsequent trials in Oyer Termiger Court: The court System for slaves.

The William A. Williams Plantation (4)

The Jacob Williams Plantation. He was the Slave Owner of Soldier Nelson (8)

The Rebecca Vaughn Plantation. This was the last battle won by the BLA (3). $25,000 grant given to Francis descendents to move and restore the house. After this victory, according to Nat Turner, "I was determined on starting for Jerusalem. Our number amounted now to fifty or sixty, all mounted and armed with guns, axes, swords and clubs."

However at the Parker Plantation, there was a sudden disagreement with a Nat Turner decision. He wanted to go immediately into Jerusalem; it was only 2 miles away. But army members used the pretext of going in to "get his men." They were jubilant and wanted to share their success with friends and family who'd been sold to Parker. Nat Turner waited at the gate. They would suffer their first defeat when they defeated a small militia, but chased them over a hillside into the arms of a larger force. The lost this battle but didn't give up.

After checking an alternative route to Jerusalem, the BLA retreated in the general direction from where they came.

It was an orderly retreat as they attempted to try to recruit more men to replenish their losses. With little success. Finally, according to Nat Turner's confession, "we stopped at Major Ridley quarter for the night. Four of his men joined us making 40 strong."

"After posting Sentinels," according to Nat Turner, "but I was quickly roused by a great racket.' There was general confusion and men and women scattered before he brought about twenty into formation. It turned out it was a false alarm. It was too late. Now there was a great need to get more men.

No doubt Nat Turner and his men were tired, but decided to push on. There was a large plantation nearby. They attacked a fortified position and suffered a horrible defeat. This was a tremendous battle the truth of which will never be fully told. But Nat Turner was reduced to two men and he sent them to look for others with orders to join him at Cabin Pond. He went ahead, but at the appointed time, according to Nat Turner. Instead of his men he saw 'white men riding around the place like they were look for somebody. At that time I knew all was lost for the present."

Nat Turner went into hiding in several safe houses he'd made in case of this eventuality.

THE FOLLOWING MEMBERS OF THE BLACK LIBERATION ARMY MEMBERS WERE TRIED AND DISPOSTITION AS INDICATED.

They were all tried in the "Slave Court" called Oyer Terminger. Nat Turner was tried in Circuit Court.

Full Trial Transcripts: Southampton County Court of Oyer and Terminer, Aug. 31-Nov. 21, 1831

Trial of Daniel (slave of Richard Porter), August 31, 1831 – Executed
Trial of Tom (slave of Caty Whitehead estate), August 31, 1831 – Discharged
Trial of Jack (slave of Caty Whitehead estate), September 1, 1831 – Transported
Trial of Andrew (slave of Caty Whitehead estate), September 1, 1831 – Transported
Trial of Moses (slave of Thomas Barrow estate), September 1, 1831 – Executed
Trial of Davy (slave of Elizabeth Turner estate), September 2, 1831 – Executed
Trial of Curtis (slave of Thomas Ridley), September 2, 1831 – Executed
Trial of Stephen (slave of Thomas Ridley), September 2, 1831 – Executed
Trial of Isaac (slave of George H. Carlton, Greenville County), September 2, 1831 – Transported
Trial of Sam (slave of Nathaniel Francis), September 3, 1831 – Executed
Trial of Hark (slave of Joseph Travis estate), September 3, 1831 – Executed
Trial of Nelson (slave of Jacob Williams), September 3, 1831 – Executed
Trial of Davy (slave of Levi Waller), September 3, 1831 – Executed
Trial of Nat (slave of Edwin Turner estate), September 3, 1831 – Executed
Trial of Jack (slave of William Reese estate), September 5, 1831 – Executed
Trial of Dred (slave of Nathaniel Francis), September 5, 1831 – Executed
Trial of Arnold Artest (free man of color), September 5, 1831 – Discharged

Trial of Nathan (slave of Benjamin Blunt estate), September 6, 1831 – Executed
Trial of Nathan, Tom, & Davy (slaves of Nathaniel Francis), September 6, 1831 –
Transported
Trial of Hardy (slave of Benjamin Edwards), September 7, 1831 – Transported
Trial of Isham (slave of Benjamin Edwards), September 7, 1831 – Transported
Trial of Sam (slave of James W. Parker), September 7, 1831 – Discharged
Trial of Jim (slave of William Vaughan), September 7, 1831 – Discharged
Trial of Bob (slave of Temperance Parker), September 8, 1831 – Discharged
Trial of Davy (slave of Joseph Parker), September 8, 1831 – Discharged
Trial of Daniel (slave of Solomon Parker), September 8, 1831 – Discharged
Trial of Joe (slave of John C. Turner), September 19, 1831 – Executed
Trial of Lucy (slave of John T. Barrow estate), September 19, 1831 – Executed
Trial of Matt (slave of Thomas Ridley), September 19, 1831 – Discharged
Trial of Thomas Haithcock (free man of color), September 19, 1831 – Superior Court
Trial of Jim (slave of Richard Porter), September 19, 1831 – Discharged
Trial of Barry Newsom (apprentice of Peter Edwards), September 20, 1831 – Superior
Court
Trial of Jack (slave of Everett Bryant), September 20, 1831 – Discharged
Trial of Exum Artist (free man of color), September 20, 1831 – Superior Court
Trial of Stephen (slave of James Bell), September 21, 1831 – Discharged
Trial of Jim & Isaac (slaves of Samuel Champion), September 22, 1831 – Transported
Trial of Preston (slave of Hannah Williamson), September 22, 1831 – Discharged
Trial of Frank (slave of Solomon Parker), September 22, 1831 – Transported
Trial of Nelson (slave of Benjamin Blunt estate), September 28, 1831 – Discharged
Trial of Jack & Shadrach (slave of Nathaniel Simmons), September 28, 1831 –
Discharged
Trial of Sam (slave of Peter Edwards), September 28, 1831 – Executed
Trial of Archer (slave of Arthur G. Reese), October 18, 1831 – Discharged
Trial of Isham Turner (free man of color), October 18, 1831 – Superior Court
Trial of Moses (slave of Joseph Travis estate), October 18, 1831 – Transported
Trial of Nat, alias Nat Turner (slave of Putnam Moore, deceased), November 5, 1831 –
Executed
Trial of Ben (slave of Benjamin Blunt estate), November 21, 1831 – Executed
Trial of Isham Turner (free man of color), October 18, 1831 – Superior Court
Trial of Moses (slave of Joseph Travis estate), October 18, 1831 – Transported
Trial of Nat, alias Nat Turner (slave of Putnam Moore, deceased), November 11, 1831 –
Executed
Trial of Ben (slave of Benjamin Blunt estate), November 21, 1831 – Executed

HAVE YOU EVER GONE THROUGH A RITES OF PASSAGE?

"Anyone who have not gone through a Rites of Passage are the Men and Women that America Wants them to be by DEFAULT"

KKVV (Khalifah Kujichagulia Village) is situated on a 123 acre tract of land that is part of the Birth Land of Nat Turner. One of the activities that we offer, in service to Black people, is a "Manup Camp Rites of Passage into Black Manhood: The following is an Application that seeks information from Black people who are interested in the Manup Camp in particular and the other activities in KKVV in general: if you have any interest, please share it with us. WHAT STATE DO YOU LIVE IN?

APPLICATION FOR THE INTERESTED: AGES 6 TO 76

What is your Name?_____

What is your Email address?_____

Do you know what a Rites of Passage is?_____

Are You interested to know more about KKVV_____

We offer Rites of Passage into Black Manhood in the following times of the year: When would you or someone that you know be likely to participate?

SPRING - SUMMER – FALL & WINTER:

SOME OTHER ACTIVITIES AT KKVV

1. Staging for Nat Turner Trail Tours
2. Nat Turner Library & Book Store
3. Nature Trials & Tours of KKVV
4. Basketball and other Recreational Sports

NAT TURNER LECTURES AVAILABLE – **Call 434-378-2140:**
SENIOR TOUR GUIDE, Elder H. Khalif Khalifah
TEAR THIS PAGE AND MAIL IT TO:
KKVV
Post Office Box 1 - Drewryville, Va. 23844

**SUGGESTED NEEDED DONATION $3.00 @
Paypal Khalifah@khabooks.com**